Jack and Jill

Instructor's Handbook

SpellingYouSee

Building Confidence

A Demme Learning Publication

Jack and Jill Instructor's Handbook

©2014 Spelling You See
©2013 Karen J. Holinga, PhD.
Published and distributed by Demme Learning

www.SpellingYouSee.com

1-888-854-6284 or +1 717-283-1448 | www.demmelearning.com
Lancaster, Pennsylvania USA

ISBN 978-1-60826-602-9

Printed in the United States of America

1   15   1014

Meet Demme Learning

Demme Learning has been providing innovative learning solutions for homeschoolers, parents, and small group learning environments since 1990. Based in Lancaster, Pennsylvania, Demme Learning is an independent family-owned and operated publishing company.

The Demme Learning family of products are designed around the involvement of an engaged parent. We recognize that engaged parents are crucial to children's success in becoming lifelong learners. Engaged parents may be primary or supplemental instructors in their child's education. Each of our products also builds on these principles:

multi-sensory instruction; sequential instruction that builds from concept to concept to achieve mastery; guided discovery; and individualized instruction that adapts to each student's unique strengths.

Visit *demmelearning.com* to learn more about us and our philosophy of education.

Meet our family of products

Math-U-See is Math You'll Love.

Math-U-See is a complete K–12 math curriculum that uses manipulatives to illustrate and teach math concepts. We "Build Understanding" in students with a multi-sensory, mastery-based approach suitable for all levels and learning styles. **Visit *mathusee.com* to learn more.**

A Unique Approach to Learning Spelling

Our program allows students to develop skills naturally, at their own pace, with the instructor's direction and encouragement. Colorful, interesting reading passages at an appropriate developmental level allow students to learn words in context, committing spelling to long-term memory. **Visit *spellingyousee.com* to learn more.**

A Parents' Guide to the Best Educational Apps for Kids

KinderTown turns your device into an educational playground with apps reviewed by childhood educators. We show only the best apps, organized by subject to easily find just what you're looking for. **Visit *kindertown.com* to learn more about our review process or to download the free app.**

The Family That Stays Together, Stays Together.

The family ministry of Steve Demme; with lectures, seminars, and books, Building Faith Families endeavors to support the key component of building lifelong learners—the engaged parent. **Visit *buildingfaithfamilies.org* to learn more.**

About Spelling You See

This innovative approach to spelling was developed by Dr. Karen Holinga, a former teacher and college professor with over 30 years of experience working with children. A qualified reading specialist, Dr. Holinga has operated a busy clinic in Ohio since 2000, helping hundreds of children become confident, successful spellers. The design of this program allows students to develop spelling skills naturally, at their own pace, supported by the direction and encouragement of the instructor.

There are no weekly spelling lists or spelling tests and no time-consuming instructor preparation. Instead, brief daily activities help students integrate writing, reading, speaking, and listening. As a result, they develop a long-term visual memory for everyday words. This prepares students for more detailed study of word patterns as they move to the advanced stages of spelling.

Visit *spellingyousee.com* for more information about Dr. Karen Holinga and Spelling You See.

Introduction

About *Jack and Jill*

Instructions for *Jack and Jill, Part 2* 26

Resources

Philosophy

"Those who set out to remember every letter of every word will never make it. Those who try to spell by sound alone will be defeated. Those who learn how to 'walk through' words with sensible expectations, noting sound, pattern, and meaning relationships, will know what to remember, and they will learn to spell English."

–EDMUND HENDERSON, 1990, p. 70

Teaching spelling can be difficult and frustrating. No matter how hard we work, and regardless of how many rules we learn, we always encounter exceptions. They are inevitable because the English language has evolved from so many different languages. We cannot consistently predict which pattern or rule will apply.

Most spelling programs are based on the premise that if children memorize a certain sequence of letters or words, they will become good spellers. The procedure is to present a word list to the children on Monday, have them study it in various ways all week, take the test on Friday, and expect them to spell each word correctly the next time they write. This approach does not work well because the brain perceives these word lists as item knowledge. Without something meaningful to connect the words to—without linkage— the brain simply reverts to rote memory, storing the words for a few days and then discarding them. The words never make it into long-term memory.

Decades ago a linguist named Charles Read (1971) noticed that preschoolers made consistent and similar assumptions about words when they were trying to figure out how to spell. From that landmark observation, numerous other researchers from the University of Virginia, headed by Edmund Henderson, confirmed and extended Read's work.

Their various studies suggested that spellers advance through a common progression, starting with sound-to-letter correspondence and moving toward more advanced and complicated spelling structures. Eventually, after years of observations and study, this group of university professors presented a model of developmental spelling based on the consistent, sequential stages through which all students move.

The developmental process of spelling is similar to what children go through when learning to walk. They need to develop the prerequisite skill of crawling before they can move on to walking and then running. In the same way, this program guides your student naturally through the stages in the process of learning to spell.

The Five Developmental Stages of Spelling

All students move through these five stages as they learn to spell:

Stage I: Preliterate

Stage II: Phonetic

Stage III: Skill Development

Stage IV: Word Extension

Stage V: Derivational Constancy

Stage I: Preliterate

Before children can read, write, or spell, they must first acquire some fundamental understandings about language. This process occurs during the preliterate stage. As children experience the printed page, both as a result of watching books being read and of exploring books on their own, they develop concepts of print. For example, they become aware that English words are written from left to right and flow from the top to the bottom of the page. Beginning writing experiences might include "pretend writing" with scribbles or random marks that eventually become more linear. Children then learn to write actual letters, often beginning with their own names, showing words as strings of letters or letter-like symbols. These activities lay the foundation for the language skills that are developed in the next stage.

Stage II: Phonetic

The second developmental stage is auditory. As children are increasingly exposed to language, they develop phonemic awareness—the ability to distinguish the individual sounds that make up spoken words in English. They then relate these sounds to print by understanding that letters represent sounds, that letters make up words, and that each word looks different.

In the phonetic stage, most instruction involves helping children match individual sounds in words to their corresponding letters, usually starting with their own names. They often use all capital letters and spell words incorrectly. For example, they may spell *KAT* for *cat*, *MI* for *my*, *LUV* for *love*, and *U* for *you*. Silent letters in words like *bake* or *lamb* may be omitted. Instructors welcome these spellings as an indication that the student is beginning to understand sound-to-letter correspondence. Children arrive at the end of the phonetic stage once they have learned the basic rules of phonics and can actively apply them to both reading and spelling.

Stage III: Skill Development

This third developmental stage is the most difficult, the most critical, and the longest for emerging spellers. It usually begins once children have cracked the basic phonetic code and are progressing rapidly in reading. As students learn the phonics rules needed to develop reading skill, they are able to apply these rules to their spelling. Problems often arise, however, when children become aware of words that are not spelled phonetically, such as *house*, *there*, and *said*. Phonics rules need to be de-emphasized at this stage because they are no longer needed to help the student learn to read. In fact, over-teaching phonics at this stage can actually create unnecessary confusion in spelling. The overriding neurological principle is that, because of the numerous inconsistencies in our language, new and different spellings must be connected to context in order for the new information to be linked correctly and permanently to long-term memory. As students encounter new vocabulary over several grade levels, spelling skill increases as they apply consistent strategies to master more complex spelling patterns and a greater number of irregularly-spelled words.

The critical thing to remember is that this is a stage—a developmental link to the stages that follow. Children are often in the skill-development stage through the fifth grade. It may seem repetitious to practice the same skills over and over again, year after year; however, if students do not master these skills, it is very difficult to move ahead in spelling development.

Stage IV: Word Extension

A much more complicated stage—the word-extension stage—focuses on syllables within words, as well as prefixes and suffixes. In the upper elementary or intermediate grades, children often struggle with issues such as doubling consonants when changing the endings (*pot/potting,* but *look/looking*) and dropping the final *e* before adding an ending (*love/loving,* but *excite/excitement*). Other issues arise with words such as *almost*. Why isn't it spelled *allmost*? Often the brightest children become the most confused or exasperated by these inconsistencies, but they eventually learn to master them as they move through this stage of development.

Stage V: Derivational Constancy

This final stage explores related words—those with the same derivation or origin— that usually have a consistent pattern despite changes in pronunciation. These words are often predictable if a student is familiar with word roots. Greek and Latin root study is helpful at this stage as mature spellers gain an understanding of how patterns and meaning are related. Students gain the most benefit from this stage if they begin derivational studies after basic vocabulary has been learned and a strong foundation has been built in the previous stages. They are often ready for this stage around seventh grade.

It is important to note that children must move through these developmental stages sequentially. Each stage builds on the previous one. Because they are developmental in nature, stages in spelling do not necessarily correspond to reading levels. In order to become a good speller in English, one must develop a strong visual memory, and for young children this can be very difficult. Even if a child excels in reading, spelling can lag far behind. It is essential that parents and teachers understand the developmental nature of the spelling process in order to guide the child effectively through the different stages.

Curriculum Sequence and Placement Guidelines

Level	Title
Level A	*Listen and Write*
Level B	*Jack and Jill*
Level C	*Wild Tales*
Level D	*Americana*
Level E	*American Spirit*
Level F	*Ancient Achievements*
Level G	*Modern Milestones*

- Do not try to match the student's reading level to an equivalent spelling level. Students must master each developmental stage of spelling before advancing to the next. Research has not established a correlation between reading achievement and spelling ability. No one can "skip" stages in spelling.

- *Listen and Write* is for a beginning reader who is learning letter names and sounds and how to hold a pencil properly when writing.

- *Jack and Jill* is for a student who prints easily with lowercase letters and knows most sounds, including long and short vowels.

- *Wild Tales* is for a student who knows all letter sounds, spells many common words correctly, and is becoming comfortable with reading.

- *Americana* is for a proficient reader with gradually improving spelling skills.

- *American Spirit* is for a student who is able to spell many common words confidently but may not be ready for the more advanced content of the next level.

- *Ancient Achievements* is for a student who is nearing the end of the Skill Development stage. It provides skill review and an introduction to the next two stages of spelling.

- *Modern Milestones* is for a student who is ready for the Word Extension stage of spelling. The student should be able to follow written directions and work independently.

- You can find detailed skill assessments for each level at spellingyousee.com.

About *Jack and Jill*

Getting Started

Overview

Jack and Jill uses a nursery rhyme theme to introduce words in an engaging yet meaningful format. This level begins with the phonetic stage of spelling and moves on to the skill-development stage. Thirty-six lessons are divided into two books for ease of use.

Needed Items

To complete the daily lessons, your student will need a regular pencil and colored pencils or highlighters (blue, green, yellow, pink or red, purple, and orange).

Using Nursery Rhymes

Nursery rhymes are part of our cultural heritage and are an ideal literary choice for this level. Their natural poetic rhythm appeals to children, and since the rhymes are usually familiar, they are perfect for readers and non-readers alike. Nursery rhymes tell a story, helping students develop an understanding of simple narrative sequences. Even when they are nonsensical, the rhymes convey powerful meaning to young children. Who can forget the cow that jumped over the moon?

Nursery rhymes provide expanded opportunities for vocabulary development because they do not have the tightly-controlled vocabulary often used at this level. Nursery rhymes introduce words and ideas that students might not otherwise hear and help students distinguish sounds that are similar, but not exactly the same. Easy to say and easy to learn, nursery rhymes add an indispensable auditory component during the phonetic and skill-development stages of spelling.

Daily Worksheet

Each of the 36 lessons is divided into five parts, A through E. One daily lesson consists of two facing pages. In the *Jack and Jill Student Workbook, Part 1*, a new nursery rhyme is read together each week. This guided reading approach helps readers of all ability levels quickly become familiar with the passage. Each day students find different details within the rhyme. Students also learn to follow directions and search for common patterns within the words, paying special attention to punctuation and capitalization.

Each day the student copies a short phrase or sentence and then fills in a set of letter boxes, focusing on short vowel sounds. The letter boxes used in *Jack and Jill, Part 1* are designed to help the brain learn sound-to-letter correspondence. The ability to make this correspondence is the most important predictor of success in reading and spelling. The neurological process of matching sounds to letters is complex, and the use of letter boxes simplifies this task. As students write each letter, they create a complete word from individual sounds. This skill is called encoding.

Jack and Jill Student Workbook, Part 2 continues the nursery rhyme theme, but now the instructor guides the student to find vowel and consonant patterns in each passage. Students also begin more extended copywork. Each day they copy a portion of the passage, stopping after 10 minutes. Then they find and mark the patterns in their own work and compare it to the passage that was marked with the instructor's help. Once a week, the student has an opportunity for creative fun with what is called "No Rule Day." The student may freely choose to write, dictate, or illustrate a response to the weekly nursery rhyme.

If all five parts of a lesson have not been completed by the end of a week, feel free to begin a new lesson the following week. Common words and letter patterns will be repeated many times throughout the course. It is more important that a student feel that he is successfully making progress than to ensure that every page is completed.

Writing Skills

In the opening lessons, correct pencil grip should be stressed. Students should use a tripod grip, holding the pencil between the thumb and the index finger as the pencil rests on the middle finger. The tripod grip establishes muscle memory and facilitates rapid writing, which in turn creates fluency.

It is also critically important that hand dominance be established. When children first begin to write, it is not unusual for them to be able to use each hand equally well. Together with your child, decide which hand will be used for writing and make sure that the same hand is used every day.

A second foundational skill emphasized throughout the first few weeks is correct letter formation. Students should write letters in one stroke (except *f, t, k, x*). Most letters should be written from the top down. See the **Handwriting Guide** (included with the student books) for more details about recommended letter formation. Single-stroke letter formation decreases the likelihood of neurological confusion. Every time a student picks up a pencil, there is an opportunity for confusion. What part of the letter comes next?

Where do I start that part? Single-stroke letter formation minimizes these unnecessary confusions which interfere with learning.

A third basic writing skill emphasized in the opening lessons is the consistent, automatic, and efficient use of lower-case letters. Since students generally begin writing in capital letters, it is prudent to avoid or break this habit before it becomes firmly entrenched. Emphasize the use of capitals to begin sentences and names. This skill will also help students as they begin the reading process. Some proper names are included in the **Daily Dictation List** to provide an opportunity to discuss the correct use of capital letters.

Correct pencil grip and correct letter formation allow for efficiency, fluency, and automaticity. When pencil grip and letter formation become automatic, the brain can handle those tasks effortlessly and concentrate on more important things, such as sound-to-letter correspondence.

At this level, students should not complete copywork in cursive. Spelling skill is the result of developing a strong visual memory. Since almost everything a student sees is in print (i. e., manuscript), it is important to maintain consistency between visual memory and writing. Most students at this level are just learning cursive, so neurological confusion is likely to result if you try to develop skills in both spelling and handwriting in the same activity. Although you want to encourage good handwriting and eventually want your student to learn cursive, do not be sidetracked by penmanship. As long as you can read what your student writes and there is appropriate space between words, focus solely on spelling, saving handwriting for its own instructional time.

Tips for Success

Use the instructions below to help you teach the skills that are the focus of each worksheet. Keep the lessons short and upbeat, offering your student as much help as needed for her to be successful. Answer keys for each lesson begin on page 58.

Online Resources

Each level has an online page with links to additional materials and resources to enhance your instructional program. You can access this page by using the password you received with this *Handbook*. If you need help accessing your online resources, please contact a Customer Service Representative.

Instructions for *Jack and Jill, Part 1*

Introduction

A day's lesson consists of two worksheets on facing pages. In *Jack and Jill Student Workbook, Part 1*, the left-hand page presents a nursery rhyme for your student to read and study. The right-hand page has letter boxes the student will use to write words from dictation. Read the directions for Lesson 1 carefully for an explanation of the rationale behind each of the exercises.

Since reading ability varies greatly at this level, you should read the nursery rhyme with your student, carefully following the directions shown on the worksheet. Each activity is purposefully planned to provide maximum benefit. For example, pointing to each word during guided reading focuses the student's attention on the letters within the word, improves eye-hand coordination, maintains left-to-right eye movement, and helps the student practice a return sweep to the next line of print. Clapping in rhythm during guided reading enables students to hear each unit of sound, or syllable, which develops the auditory memory necessary for accurate spelling.

In most cases, the same rhyme is used for all five worksheets in each lesson. This is intentional. As students become more familiar with the passage, non-phonetic and high-frequency sight words will become impressed on the visual memory, enabling the students to spell them more accurately in their independent writing. Guide your student in answering the questions under the passage. Students may be directed to underline specific words or to circle letters or marks of punctuation. Later, colored pencils or highlighters will be used for specific spelling patterns.

The right-hand page of each lesson provides letter boxes in which your student can practice writing words. For the first two lessons, the student will copy the words. Starting in Lesson 3, students will write the words that you dictate. The **Daily Dictation List** begins on page 43 of this *Handbook*.

Lesson 1: Rhyming, Details in Print, Short *a*

- Read the passage on the left-hand page together, following the directions carefully. For the first six lessons in the workbook, each word in the passage begins with a letter in bold type. This will help your student identify individual word units as she reads.

- Have the student copy the given words on the lines provided at the bottom of the first page.

- The right-hand page focuses on letter formation and the short *a* sound. Start by having the student practice writing the letters given at the top of each page. Then have him trace the three-letter words in the letter boxes and copy each word in the second row of boxes. Insist that the student say the sound of the letter, not the name of the letter, as each one is written. Saying the sound coordinates the visual (seeing the letter), kinesthetic (writing the letter), and auditory (hearing the sound), and makes a neurological connection between the letter and its sound.

Lesson 2: Rhyming, Details in Print, Short *i*

- Carefully follow the directions on the left-hand page for reading the rhyme together. Answer the questions.

- Even though the words on the right-hand page are given for the student to trace, read each word to the student and have the student say the sound of each letter. Then have the student read each word back to you, giving as much help as is needed.

- Feel free to move to a new lesson each week, even if you have not finished all the pages in your current lesson. Words and sounds will be repeated.

Lesson 3: Introduce Dictation, Details in Print, Short *o*

- This is the first lesson with dictation. Before introducing dictation, take a moment to relax the student. Be positive and encouraging! You want to build confidence and promote success.

- Explain to the student that instead of tracing or copying words in the letter boxes, she will begin writing the words you say. Be sure to tell the student what vowel or vowels she will be working on each day.

- Using the **Daily Dictation List** that begins on page 43, slowly and clearly read each word. Students should say the sound as they write each letter. Do not overlook this critical step.

- Don't be afraid to help your student. Anticipate where a problem might occur and guide the student through the difficult parts. If he struggles with the difference between *b* and *d*, for example, show him how to write the correct letter. Encourage him to ask if he is not sure whether *cut* starts with *c* or *k*. On the other hand, try to give only as much help as needed. Students should feel a sense of accomplishment in being able to work independently.

- Limit the time spent on dictation to no more than 10 minutes a day. Do not pressure a child to write more than he or she can accomplish comfortably in that amount of time.

- You may want to read more about **Letter Box Dictation** on page 37 to prepare for these lessons.

- Worksheet 3C asks you and your student to find words with three syllables. (Example: *happily*.) A syllable is a word or part of a word pronounced as a single unit. It consists of one vowel sound and often the consonant sounds that cluster around it. When you clap the words together, each syllable should be represented by one clap.

Lesson 4: Details in Print, Reading the Words Back, Short *u*

- Some of the directions for the nursery rhyme are a little different this week. On worksheet 4C, your student will be asked to find all of the *-ed* endings and mark them in pink or red using a colored pencil or highlighter. We are beginning to teach a color code for different letter groups that will be used throughout the curriculum. You can find a complete guide to this process, called "chunking," on page 33. Other questions in this lesson involve recognizing vocabulary and meaning. Give the student as much help as he needs–this is not a test!

- Insist that your student read each word back after dictation if she is not doing so already. When a student sounds out a word letter-by-letter in order to read it back, she is practicing the skill of decoding. Decoding is a completely different neurological task than encoding, and the brain must be able to do both. When students understand that they have to read the words back at the end of dictation, they think about each word more carefully as they write each letter and say each sound. If we do not ask students to do this, they will not process the words in the same careful way.

- Beginning readers may struggle to read words back. Read the words together until your student feels comfortable reading them alone.

Lesson 5: Details in Print, Counting the Correct Words, Short *e*

- As your student studies this week's rhyme, he will be asked to notice quotation marks, number words, and opposites, as well as capital letters and punctuation.

- Worksheet 5D asks students to notice words that rhyme but have different spelling patterns. This is very important. We want students to begin to process words visually, not just phonetically.

- Beginning in this lesson, each dictation page has a line where your student can record the number of words that were spelled correctly. Notice that we record the number of correct words, not the number of incorrect words. It is important to keep the dictation experience positive for your student. Ideally, she should get each word correct with guidance and help.

Lesson 6: Details in Print, Review of Short *a*, *e*, *i*, *o*, and *u*

- In this lesson the student will be looking for two different word endings. It is important that the student use pink or red to mark all word endings. A new punctuation mark is also introduced in this lesson. Be sure to read the questions carefully on each day's worksheet.

- In this lesson, the words for dictation feature all five short vowel sounds. There are no letters in the boxes to give hints. If your student has difficulty with this, you may choose words with the same vowel sound and use them over and over to build confidence and speed. The **General Dictation List** on page 46 organizes words by sounds or letter patterns.

Lesson 7: Details in Print, Vowel Review

- Continue to follow the directions for the guided reading of each nursery rhyme as explained on the worksheets. This process is very important in helping students develop a visual memory for words with a wide variety of spelling patterns.

- The right-hand page has boxes for 12 words instead of six. Remember that dictation should be completed in about 10 minutes, so feel free to stop at the end of that time. Have your student read the words back and record the number of words that were spelled correctly. Move on to the next worksheet on the next day.

Lesson 8: Details in Print, Beginning Blends with Short *a*

- The student is asked to find and mark four different vowels this week.

- Beginning blends and words with four letters are introduced in this lesson. Explain that the third box in each word is shaded to show exactly where to write the vowel. Point out the pattern of each word: two consonants followed by a vowel and then a consonant at the end.

- A blend is made up of two (or more) individual consonant sounds blended together, as in *stop* or *brim*. However, in this dictation exercise, while the student is still learning sound-to-letter correspondence, he needs to hear and be aware of each individual sound. Articulate each of the four sounds in each word so that he can hear them as four separate sounds. Do not blend the sounds together as you dictate the word. As he writes each letter, he must also say each sound individually.

- The words used for dictation in Lesson 8 all have the short *a* sound so that the student can concentrate on the sounds of the letters that make up the blends.

Lesson 9: Details in Print, Chunking, Blends with Short *i*

- In this lesson, students are introduced to a process known as "chunking." This is the process of marking particular letter patterns according to the directions given in each lesson.

- Chunking is a central element in subsequent levels of this program, as the physical practice of marking chunks not only helps students focus on details in print but also helps the brain identify letter patterns within words.

- On 9B, "Bossy *r* chunks" are introduced. When a vowel is followed by an *r*, the vowel sound changes, or "the *r* bosses the vowel." Have your student use a purple pencil or highlighter to mark the Bossy *r* chunks. There is a detailed guide to chunking on page 33.

- Write the following word pairs for your student to read: *cat-car, bed-her, sit-sir, hot-for, pup-purr*. Point out how the vowel makes its regular short sound in the first word but changes in the second word as it is affected by the *r*.

- On worksheet 9C, students are asked to find and mark silent *e*. Silent *e* should be marked in orange.

- Continue to limit the time spent on dictation to 10 minutes a day. The words used for dictation for the first three days all have the short *i* sound. On the last two days of this lesson, dictation will review short *a* and short *i*.

Lesson 10: Details in Print, Blends with Short *o*, Recording Time

- Continue to follow the directions on the student worksheets carefully as you and your student look for word patterns and other details.

- Beginning in Lesson 10, some dictation worksheets include a line to record the student's time. When teaching letters and sounds, the immediate purpose is not primarily to learn specific words; it is to help students understand sound-to-letter correspondence so that they are able to encode and decode words easily. Timing the exercise encourages students to process words quickly, automatically, and effortlessly. The focus is not on spelling the words themselves but on the neurological process behind the spelling.

- Timing the dictation makes the exercise more of a game as your student works harder and faster to beat his time. As he writes words more quickly and easily, he solidifies his encoding skills. However, do not insist on timing the dictation if it causes frustration for your student.

- If your student is struggling during dictation, use the same words over and over to build confidence and speed. A **General Dictation List** is provided on page 46 if you choose to do extra review or focus on specific sounds.

Lesson 11: Vowel Chunks, Beginning Blends with Short *u*

- Continue to read the passages together as directed. This is very important—we want students to concentrate on the details of the passage using both their eyes and their ears.

- Your student will mark vowel chunks for the first time on worksheet 11A. Have the student use a yellow pencil or highlighter for vowel chunks. There is a complete list of vowel chunks on page 33.

- On worksheet 11E, your student is asked to mark the silent *l* in the word *walk*. Your student may notice that the sound of the vowel in words such as *walk* or *could* changes when it is followed by an *l*. In this case the *l* acts like a "Bossy *l*," but since it is still silent, it should be marked in orange.

- The entire dictation exercise should not take more 10 minutes. Stop after that time and move on to the next worksheet on the next day.

Lesson 12: Details in Print, Beginning Blends with Short *e*

- Carefully follow the directions for marking each passage. The *rr* consonant chunk will be new this week.

- On dictation worksheet 12D, the vowels will not be given for the student. If your student is not sure of the correct vowel, tell her rather than letting her guess. Be sure that she says each sound as she writes the letters.

Lesson 13: Tricky *y* Guy, Digraphs

- "Tricky *y* Guy" is new this week. It is usually found at the end of words but may be in the middle as well. Tricky *y* Guy can sound like long *e* (*baby*), long *i* (*fly*), or short *i* (*bicycle*). When *y* is the first letter of either a word or a syllable, it is not "tricky." Instead, it keeps its regular consonant sound. Use green to mark Tricky *y* Guy.

- A digraph is a combination of two letters that make a single unique sound. The words used for dictation in this lesson include the digraphs *th*, *ch*, and *sh*. Most students have already seen these combinations in phonics lessons or encountered them in sight words. However, you should take some time to explain that the two letters together make a special sound. When writing the words, the student should say the sound of the combination, rather than the sounds of the individual letters. Be sure to give as much help as needed for this new step.

Lesson 14: Tricky *y* Guy, Bossy *r*, End Blends, and Digraphs

- Carefully follow the directions for each worksheet. Be sure to use the correct color for each letter combination.

- Beginning in this lesson, students will work on writing words that have the vowel in the second position and a blend or digraph at the end of the word. Before you begin dictation, draw your student's attention to this new pattern: one consonant, one vowel in the shaded box, and two consonants.

- 14D highlights the punctuation mark called a colon. In this passage the colon introduces a list.

Lesson 15: *Ck* and Double Consonants

- Continue the guided reading of each passage as explained in the instructions. This focused attention to detail will improve both reading and spelling skills.

- The dictation for this week introduces words with *ck* or double consonants at the end. Be sure to tell your student about the new letter combinations before you begin dictation.

- On page 15E, there are no shaded vowel boxes on the dictation pages. The vowel may go in either the second or third box. Provide as much help as your student needs.

Lesson 16: Details in Print, Beginning and End Blends

- The student will be asked to mark the *-ing* ending and other letter patterns in this lesson. Be consistent about using the same color for each element.

- There are no shaded vowel boxes on the dictation pages for this lesson. Provide as much help as your student needs. Stop dictation after 10 minutes and count the number of words that are spelled correctly.

Lesson 17: Details in Print, Words with Five Letters

- Encourage your student to work as independently as possible when finding the different letter combinations. At the same time, give help as needed. The pages are not tests!

- The dictation pages in this lesson feature words with five letters. The middle box is shaded to show where the vowel should be written.

Lesson 18: Details in Print, Words with Five Letters

- This is the last lesson in *Jack and Jill Student Workbook, Part 1*. Be sure to celebrate your student's accomplishment.

- This will be the last lesson to use letter boxes. There are no shaded boxes for vowels. If you feel that your student needs more practice with vowel sounds or blends, consult the **General Dictation List** on page 46. If you give extra practice with dictation, be sure to limit the practice to 10 minutes at a time.

Instructions for *Jack and Jill, Part 2*

Introduction

Jack and Jill Student Workbook, Part 2 continues the nursery rhyme format, and the daily worksheets still consist of two pages. In this book, students will continue to "chunk" a variety of letter combinations. Copywork sections are longer, and the student will begin to write whole sentences from dictation. There will also be opportunities for free writing or drawing in response to the passage. As before, feel free to move to a new lesson each week, even if the previous lesson was not completed. Common words and letter patterns will be repeated many times.

On the fourth day of each lesson, your student has the opportunity for creative self-expression. As he responds to the nursery rhymes, he can explore different forms of communication, including narrating, writing, and illustrating. Students at this age may have limited writing skills but not limited imaginations. "No Rule Day" offers a chance for their imaginations to soar as they write or dictate or illustrate. We encourage parents not to correct or grade these artistic expressions. As a result, your student is more likely to enjoy the writing experience while he becomes comfortable with the process. There are more suggestions for **No Rule Day** on page 36.

On the last day of the week, you will dictate the passage for your student to write. When you start passage dictation, relax the student and tell her not to worry; you will provide all punctuation and capitalization and help her with difficult words. You will do this for just 10 minutes—no more! Read the passage slowly, word by word, until your student struggles with a word. Stop to help, but don't stop the clock. It is important to address misspellings as they occur without worrying about time. When 10 minutes are up, stop and count the number of words written correctly. You can read more important information about **Passage Dictation** on page 38.

Lesson 19: Vowel Chunks, Copywork

- Continue to read the passage together following the steps you used in *Jack and Jill Student Workbook, Part 1*. This is an important way to help your student focus visually on each word.

- The student will be looking for and marking vowel chunks for this entire lesson. The vowel chunks are listed on each left-hand page as an aid to the student and the instructor. There is a complete **Guide to Chunking** starting on page 33. Have the student mark the vowel chunks in yellow. Give as much help as needed and remember that this will get easier with practice.

- On the first three days of the lesson, move on to the right-hand page and have your student copy as much as he can complete in 10 minutes. After the 10 minutes are up, the student should "chunk" his work (mark the vowel chunks), looking at the opposite page if needed.

- On the fourth day of the lesson, the right hand page has room for the student to write her own story or draw her own picture. On the fifth day, you will be dictating the nursery rhyme for your student to write. Go to page 38 in this *Handbook* for more detailed instructions about **Passage Dictation**.

Lesson 20: Vowel Chunks, Silent Letters

- In this lesson, you and your student will continue to look for vowel chunks and mark them in yellow. Because the letters *w* and *y* act like vowels, they are included in some of the vowel chunks.

- You are also directed to look for silent letters that are not part of chunks. A silent *e* is often found at the end of a word, but there may also be a silent *b* or *h* in a word. Words like *thumb* or *oh* can be tricky. Mark the silent letters in orange. When directed to chunk the passage, include both vowel chunks and silent letters.

- When guiding dictation, do not tell the student to "sound out" a word. Instead, you can remind her of another word that has the same letter combination. For example, *road* has the same vowel chunk as *boat*. Remember to limit the time spent on dictation to 10 minutes.

Lesson 21: Vowel Chunks, Tricky *y* Guy

- Continue to look for vowel chunks and mark them in yellow.

- You will also be looking for Tricky *y* Guy in this lesson. Tricky *y* Guy is usually found at the end of a word. It can sound like long *e*, short *i*, or long *i*. Words like *bicycle* can have a Tricky *y* in the middle. Mark Tricky *y* Guy in green.

- When completing copywork or dictation, do not get sidetracked with penmanship. As long as you can read what the student writes and there is appropriate spacing between words, focus on spelling. Save penmanship practice for another time.

Lesson 22: Bossy *r* Chunks

- This lesson will focus on Bossy *r* chunks. When a vowel (*a, e, i, o, u*) is followed by an *r*, the vowel sound changes. Look at the directions for Lesson 9 in this *Handbook* to review how *r* changes the sound of a vowel. Mark Bossy *r* chunks in purple.

- When the 10 minutes of dictation are up, the student should count the number of words that are spelled correctly and record that number at the top of the page. Be positive; always consider the number right, not the number wrong. It may help to be generous as well. It is fine for students to count the words provided at the beginning of the dictation lines.

Lesson 23: Vowel Chunks

- This lesson will focus on vowel chunks. Always mark vowel chunks in yellow.

- Check your student's work on the left-hand page before she begins the copywork on 23A, 23B, and 23C. When the copywork is finished, have her mark all the vowel chunks, using the opposite page as a reference if needed.

Lesson 24: Vowel Chunks, Bossy *r* Chunks

- This lesson reviews both vowel chunks and Bossy *r* chunks. Have your student mark the vowel chunks first in yellow and then go back and mark Bossy *r* chunks in purple.

- No Rule Day is an opportunity to develop student interest in writing, listening, storytelling, and illustrating. Allow your student to be creative while keeping the time spent to about 10 minutes, unless the student wants to continue.

Lesson 25: Vowel Chunks, Bossy *r* Chunks

- Don't forget to read the poem together as directed. Multiple readings build visual memory and syllable awareness.

- By now, your student should be comfortable with finding the chunks in this lesson. Even so, be prepared to give as much help as he needs.

Lesson 26: Consonant Chunks

- In this lesson, the student will be looking for consonant chunks. They should be marked in blue. Point out that a consonant chunk may change the sounds of the letters or be silent. For example, *gh* becomes silent in several words in this lesson. Be prepared to spend a little more time helping your student until he becomes familiar with the consonant chunks.

- No Rule Day suggestion: Have your student dictate a story to you. Then she can illustrate it or use one or two sentences as copywork.

Lesson 27: Consonant Chunks

- In this lesson the student is still working with consonant chunks. Mark them in blue. There is a complete guide to all of the chunks used in this program beginning on page 33.

- When the student is chunking his own copywork, it is fine to refer to the opposite page for help.

Lesson 28: Consonant Chunks, Endings

- This lesson adds some common word endings to the letter combinations to be marked. Use pink or red to mark the endings.

- No Rule Day suggestion: Single out one word in the rhyme and illustrate it, using markers, glitter, stencils, or other art materials.

Lesson 29: Consonant Chunks, Tricky *y* Guy

- In addition to consonant chunks, you will also be looking for Tricky *y* Guy in this lesson. Remind your student that Tricky *y* Guy is usually found at the end of a word, but words like *bicycle* can have a Tricky *y* in the middle. It can sound like long *e*, short *i*, or long *i*. Mark Tricky *y* Guy in green.

- Don't forget that you and your student should be finding and marking the letter combinations together. Use the answer key to be sure you have found all the combinations.

- Continue to keep dictation day relaxed. Dictate slowly and give as much help as is needed. Stop after 10 minutes and count the number of correct words. Celebrate progress.

Lesson 30: Vowel and Consonant Chunks

- In this lesson your student will be asked to mark both vowel and consonant chunks. Remember to use yellow for the vowels and blue for the consonants.

- There is an apostrophe at the beginning of the word *'twas*. It shows us that the letter *i* was left out to make a short form of *it was*.

- During a dictation session, do not read the whole passage quickly and then go back and check for misspelled words. It is better to complete only a few sentences, word by word, and walk your student through the process of creating visual connections. The goal is quality, not quantity. It is more beneficial for your student to write each word correctly than to write many words incorrectly. The number of words that can be written correctly in 10 minutes will increase with experience.

Lesson 31: Consonant Chunks and Silent Letters

- In this lesson, you and your student will continue to look for consonant chunks and mark them in blue.

- You are also directed to look for silent letters that are not part of chunks. A silent *e* is often found at the end of a word. There is also a silent *b* in this passage. Mark the silent letters in orange. Notice that the *kn* is marked as a consonant chunk, so the *k* does not need to be marked again as a silent letter.

- Remember to relax on No Rule Day. Allow your student to choose an activity that he enjoys each time. See page 36 for ideas. Don't correct these activities.

Lesson 32: Consonant Chunks and Silent Letters

- This lesson provides another opportunity to practice marking consonant chunks and silent letters in the same passage. Consonant chunks are always marked in blue, while silent letters are marked in orange. Insist that your student always use the same color for each kind of letter pattern.

- Remember that copywork is very important in helping students learn our language. Students take words in visually and then copy them kinesthetically. Throughout the process, they also must pay close attention to details in print that might otherwise elude them. Copywork acts as a cognitive structuring device, sorting information visually so it is more easily organized and processed by the brain. Do not skip or minimize this activity.

Lesson 33: Consonant Chunks, Silent Letters, and Tricky *y* Guy

- When the student is directed to "chunk" a rhyme, she should mark all the letter patterns mentioned in the lesson. Even though silent letters and Tricky *y* Guy are not technically chunks, they should be marked in this lesson as part of the chunking process. Be sure to provide all the help that is needed as your student chunks three different letter patterns in this lesson.

- Tricky *y* Guy is usually found at the end of a word. It can sound like long *e*, short *i*, or long *i*. Words like *bicycle* can have a Tricky *y* in the middle. Mark Tricky *y* Guy in green. There is a complete guide to chunking on page 33.

- From now on, two pages are provided in the student book for the dictation activity. Even though these passages are a little longer, continue to limit the time spent on dictation to 10 minutes.

Lesson 34: Vowel Chunks, Tricky *y* Guy

- The focus of this lesson is vowel chunks and Tricky *y* Guy. Vowel chunks are marked in yellow and Tricky *y* Guy in green.

- Always check the chunked passage for correctness before having the student copy and chunk the passage on the right-hand page. The original passage can then be used as a reference as the student works.

Lesson 35: Vowel Chunks, Tricky *y* Guy, and Endings

- You and your student looked for vowel chunks and Tricky *y* Guy in the last lesson. In this lesson, you will review those letters and also look for and mark word endings. The word endings that you are to look for are given in a box on each lesson page. Mark each ending in pink or red.

- The letter groups *est* and *en* are not listed as endings because those letter combinations appear in many words as part of the base word. Two examples are the words *west* and *ten*.

- Go to page 35 for more information on how to work with letter chunks that seem to overlap. Remember that the goal of chunking is to help students look closely at words and notice different spelling patterns. If your student marked the chunks differently than the answer key, discuss the possibility of there being more than one way to mark the word. The student will have met the goal of focusing on spelling patterns even if the words are marked somewhat differently than in the answer key.

Lesson 36: Consonant Chunks, Bossy *r* Chunks, and Silent Letters

- There are three different letter patterns to be marked in this lesson. Be sure to use the correct color for each one. (Note: The letter *q* is nearly always followed by *u*. We opted to put *qu* in the category of consonant chunks.)

- After completing this week's dictation page, let your student compare it with a page from the first part of the course. Do you see improvement in the number of words spelled correctly? Take time to celebrate your student's progress.

Guide to Chunking

In *Jack and Jill Student Workbook, Part 1*, students are casually introduced to a process known as "chunking a passage," which is a central element in subsequent levels of this program. The word "chunk" refers to a specific letter combination that the student is asked to find and mark. Be sure to use the suggested color for each kind of letter pattern.

In *Jack and Jill Student Workbook, Part 2*, students begin chunking the passage each day, locating and marking specific patterns within the words of the weekly nursery rhyme. At first the chunking process is fairly simple. Students search for one particular kind of letter pattern, or chunk, such as a vowel chunk or consonant chunk. Gradually, students are challenged to find and mark multiple spelling patterns in each passage. Students should use colored pencils or highlighters to chunk the passages. The use of color simplifies the process of counting different patterns and adds an element of fun to the search.

The various letter groups are listed below, along with the color that should be used to mark each group.

Vowel Chunks (yellow)

aa ae ai ao au aw ay

ea ee ei eo eu ew ey eau

ia ie ii io iu

oa oe oi oo ou ow oy

ua ue ui uo uu uy

- Notice that the three-letter combination *eau* is included in this list.
- Because the letters *w* and *y* can act like vowels, they are also included in some of the vowel chunks.
- Even if each vowel sound is articulated in a vowel pair, as in *radio* or *area*, the pair should be marked as a vowel chunk.

Consonant Chunks (blue)

ch	gh	ph	sh	th	wh		
wr	gn	kn	dg	qu	ck	tch	
bb	cc	dd	ff	gg	hh	kk	ll
mm	nn	pp	rr	ss	tt	ww	vv	zz

- Notice that the three-letter combination *tch* is included in this list.

- The chunk *qu* is a consonant-vowel combination that we have chosen to include with the consonant chunks.

- The letter pairs *tw* (*two*) and *sc* (*science*) are treated as blends rather than consonant chunks because they usually are sounded individually (*twig, scope*).

- The combination *mb* is not considered a consonant chunk because each letter is part of a different syllable in many English words (*combine, steamboat*).

Bossy *r* Chunks (purple)

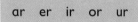

ar   er   ir   or   ur

- Notice how the *r* changes the sound of the vowel in the following word pairs: *cat-car, bed-her, sit-sir, hot-for, pup-purr.*

- There are some words (*cupboard, their, your*) that have a vowel chunk overlapped by a Bossy *r* chunk. If a student is marking both vowel chunks and Bossy *r* chunks in a lesson, we suggest marking the vowel chunk first.

- If there is a Bossy *r* chunk before a consonant chunk (*stirrup, hurry*), we suggest marking the Bossy *r* chunk.

Tricky *y* Guy (green)

- Tricky *y* Guy is usually found at the end of words but may be in the middle. It can sound like long *e* (*baby*), long *i* (*fly*), or short *i* (*bicycle*).

Endings (pink or red)

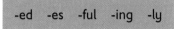

- If the student marks *-ly* as an ending in a word like *only*, do not mark it wrong, even though it is not technically an ending added to a base word. Base words and endings are included in advanced word study.

- The *est* and *en* letter combinations frequently appear as part of a base word (*west*, *ten*). They have not been listed as endings.

- In words such as *doing* and *being*, we suggest marking the endings rather than vowel chunks when the student is looking for both patterns.

Silent Letters (orange)

- Silent *e* is often found at the end of words. Some words have a silent *b* (*thumb*) or silent *h* (*oh*).

- The *l* in some words (*walk, could*) is silent. Notice that the *l* in *walk* controls the vowel sound of the *a* that precedes it.

- Only silent letters that are not part of chunks should be marked.

Overlapping Chunks

Some words have overlapping chunks. In words where the final *y* is changed to *i* before adding an ending (*studied, countries*), marking either the ending or the vowel chunk is acceptable. The word *finally* has a consonant chunk (*ll*) and an ending (*-ly*) that overlap. If the focus of the lesson is consonant chunks, students should chunk *ll*. If the focus is endings, students should chunk *-ly*.

Some lessons ask the student to mark multiple chunks. The purpose of chunking is to train the student to look carefully at how words are spelled. If he chooses a different combination of letters than in the answer key, do not mark it wrong. Discuss his choice and point out other possibilities. Your student may find it helpful to chunk the letter combination that he thinks will be the most difficult to remember.

No Rule Day

No Rule Day is an opportunity to develop your student's interest in writing, listening, storytelling, and illustrating. Allow your student to be creative. Resist the temptation to correct spelling or penmanship. The goal is to encourage the free expression of ideas and imagination in a fun and relatively painless way.

Writing is not an easy skill to master. This activity offers a chance for students to write without worry or pressure. It is not meant to be drudgery, so don't require more than 10 minutes unless the student wants to continue. Below are some simple ideas for your student to try.

- Draw something related to the weekly nursery rhyme. Focus on a character, setting, event, or result.

- Write one sentence about the weekly nursery rhyme.

- Dictate a story to the instructor. Then illustrate it, read it aloud, or use the story as copywork.

- Choose one word in the rhyme and illustrate it. Use markers, colored pencils, glitter, a stencil, or other art materials.

- Change the ending of the rhyme. Explain and/or illustrate the new ending.

- Ask *why*. "Why did the mouse run up the clock?" "Why did Humpty Dumpty fall?" Write or illustrate an answer to the question.

- Ask *how*. "How did the old man come rolling home?" Write or illustrate your answer to the question.

- Ask *what*. "What did the poor dog have to eat instead of a bone?" Write or illustrate your answer.

- Think of other words that rhyme with the last words in the lines of the poem. Write or dictate new lines that either change the rhyme or add to it.

Letter Box Dictation

Many young children demonstrate immature articulation. This is especially true for children who have auditory processing delays or who have had a history of ear infections. For these children, the process of learning sound-to-letter correspondence can be especially challenging. However, the more difficult this process is, the more critical it is that they learn it.

The sounds of *g, j,* and *h,* as well as *tr, dr,* and *ch* may be especially difficult. During the dictation exercise, students may make substitutions in words with these sounds. You may notice them writing *jrep* for the word *drip, gob* for *job,* or *chrap* for *trap.* When this occurs, take the time to demonstrate exactly how you make the sound. Use the same words over and over until they are no longer confused.

Final blends and digraphs (*ch, sh, th*) can also be difficult and are often written incompletely. A special type of omission occurs with nasal consonants *m* and *n* before another consonant. Students may write *bop* instead of *bump* and *lad* instead of *land.*

If the dictation in *Jack and Jill Student Workbook, Part 1* is labor-intensive and the student is struggling, it may be beneficial to use the same words repeatedly to build the student's confidence and speed. This is not cheating. Your student must feel successful. Let him leave with a smile on his face and feeling good about what he has just accomplished. Do whatever you need to do to make the dictation exercise fun and easy. Be patient and stay positive. The most important thing is solid understanding, not how much you accomplish in any given day or how quickly you cover the material.

Passage Dictation

Passage dictation is not a stand-alone activity. Students should always chunk the passage first. They are learning how to learn, how to store information, how to create links, and how to remember. This sets them up for success. Neurologically, students have to be relaxed, engaged, and motivated. Consider dictation a game or challenge. Be positive and always consider the number of words spelled correctly, not the number spelled incorrectly.

When you start dictation, tell the student to relax and not worry. You will provide all punctuation and capitalization and help with difficult words. The dictation will last for only 10 minutes. Read the passage word by word until your student needs assistance. Stop to help, but don't stop the clock. It is important to address misspellings as they occur without worrying about time. It is more beneficial for students to write each word correctly than to write many words incorrectly. Gradually dictation will become easier, and eventually your student will write more words correctly each week.

Discuss the non-phonetic word parts—"the rule breakers"—as you go. For example, show students how "tricky" the *gh* chunk is. This consonant chunk appears in words like *light*, *enough*, and *ghost*. *Ugh*! The *ai* chunk appears in *rain*, *again*, and *captain*. The word *house* has a silent *e* at the end. This is why it is not helpful to tell students to "sound it out." When we show them that the rules are inconsistent, we relieve them of the burden of figuring out why a word is spelled a certain way. Their brains are then free to visualize the word in context and to retrieve that visual image from memory.

High-frequency words are often the most difficult to spell. Students will learn them through repeated use in context. Explain to your student that her paper is "sloppy copy" and that she does not need to erase. Students sometimes have to write words several ways before they pinpoint the one that looks right, so let them compare different spellings. You may prompt her, "Try it with and without an *e* at the end." Have her draw a line through the wrong words and keep going. (Note that students can and should erase on their copywork, if needed.)

Once students begin to grasp spelling patterns, reading becomes easier as well, and the brain starts to identify patterns within new words through context. Rather than using rote memorization or constantly trying to figure out which rule applies, students simply need to ask themselves, "What did that word that I copied all week look like?" Over time, the brain starts to connect the letter patterns and create linkage to other words with the same patterns. Eventually students will link *rain* to *said* as they make the visual connection.

Frequently Asked Questions

1. **Are students allowed to ask for help?**

   Yes. It is a very positive step when students articulate their questions. Encourage your student to ask if he is confused by something. For example, if he isn't sure if *cab* starts with *c* or *k*, have him ask rather than write the word incorrectly. If he struggles with *b* and *d*, simply show him how to write the correct letter. You want your student to succeed, so help him. Eliminate opportunities for mistakes. It is better for a student to have the visual image of the correct letter or word rather than an incorrect one.

2. **My child doesn't seem to be making progress. Do you have any suggestions?**

   Some students have trouble hearing sounds clearly, possibly because of auditory processing delays or a history of ear infections. No matter what the reason for slow progress, do not be tempted to skip ahead. Especially at the beginning, it may help to use the same few words several times until the student understands the dictation process. Instead of following the **Daily Dictation List**, continue to repeat words from previous days. Using more familiar words increases student confidence and improves speed. You may also select words from the **General Dictation List** if your student needs extra practice with specific sounds or blends.

3. **Some programs use nonsense words to make sure students know the sounds that letters make. Can I use nonsense words in the letter boxes?**

   The use of nonsense words is not recommended. Meaning drives the brain. In order for students to learn critical encoding and decoding skills, they need experience with actual words that make sense.

4. **My child gets upset when I head for the timer. Is it really necessary to time the dictation exercise?**

   Timing is a motivational tool to help students increase their speed. Some students love trying to beat their time. If your child resists, skip the timing. Do keep in mind that students should write words more quickly and confidently over time. If your child enjoys being timed, but his handwriting deteriorates during the timed exercise, don't worry as long as you can read his writing. Save handwriting practice for another time.

5. **By the time my child finishes writing words in the letter boxes, he doesn't want to read the words back. Can we just skip that step?**

    Reading words back is a critical part of the program. When students write a word, they encode it as they make the sound-to-letter correspondence. When they read the word back, they decode it, which is like reconstructing the word. Students often find decoding more difficult than encoding, but both of these distinct skills are indispensable.

6. **Should my student erase during copywork?**

    Students should erase during copywork if necessary, so that they are practicing the words correctly.

7. **Should my student erase during passage dictation?**

    When students are completing dictation, it is important not to erase. Give your student the chance to write the word multiple times, if needed, in order to see which one looks right. Simply have him draw a line through the incorrect words.

8. **Should I keep a list of words that my student misses?**

    No, this is not necessary. Commonly misspelled words will come up again in future lessons. This program encourages visual memory, not rote memory.

9. **We didn't have time to do spelling every day this week. Is it important to finish every worksheet?**

    While it is important to work on spelling consistently, it should not be a burden to you or your student. Feel free to start a new lesson each week even if the previous lesson was not completed. The common words and letter patterns will be repeated many times throughout the course.

10. **There are no spelling tests with this program. How can I tell if my child is making progress?**

    Look for increased accuracy and the ability to complete pages more quickly. You should also see more accurate spelling in other daily work. However, remember that each child will progress through the developmental process at his or her own pace, so be patient and do not put pressure on your student. Also keep in mind that creative writing uses a different part of the brain and may continue to contain more spelling errors than the dictation exercises for some time. Eventually the correct spelling will become automatic.

    If you are required or would like to keep a portfolio of your student's work, pages may be removed from the workbooks at regular intervals and kept in a folder.

Resources

Daily Dictation List

For *Jack and Jill Student Workbook, Part 1,* we have included a word list for ease of instruction. This list is not intended to be lengthy or exhaustive. The words provided are simply a means to an end: developing strong phonemic awareness, which will equip students with the ability to encode and decode words as they progress in both spelling and reading.

The **Daily Dictation List** is designed to provide a helpful option that will simplify lesson preparation and correspond to the lesson focus. Also available is the **General Dictation List** sorted by vowel sounds, beginning blends, and so on. If students need extra practice with a specific vowel sound, for example, you may want to use words from the general list rather than the daily list. Both options are available so you can adapt the program to fit the needs of your student.

Please note: In the letter boxes we never use words that have a vowel followed by *r* (*car, stir, blur*). The *r* changes the sound of the vowel, which can confuse students who are still trying to understand sound-to-letter correspondence. After all, *er, ir,* and *ur* all sound the same! This letter pattern will be addressed later in *Jack and Jill.*

1A	**1B**	**1C**	**1D**	**1E**
cat gas dad	jam sad dad	can sag had	jab lag ram	wax tag nap
cat gas dad	jam sad dad	can sag had	jab lag ram	wax tag nap

2A	**2B**	**2C**	**2D**	**2E**
nip bin fix	bid lip him	fig sit rib	fin rip him	nip fib win
nip bin fix	bid lip him	fig sit rib	fin rip him	nip fib win

3A	**3B**	**3C**	**3D**	**3E**
box not mop	got fox pod	lot mom cob	lop cot sob	job hog dot
sob dog rot	mob Bob hog	nod top dog	fog hop pox	mom rod Bob

4A	**4B**	**4C**	**4D**	**4E**
rub hum pun	bun gum tub	fun lug Gus	bug sun cut	bus cud mug
bud nut mug	cup mug hut	bus rut pup	mud rug hum	gum sub pup

5A	**5B**	**5C**	**5D**	**5E**
men fed keg	pen led beg	ten yet bed	fed net yes	Ted web get
yes hem pet	get web red	wed keg vet	pen red jet	leg pen red

6A
hog dig ham
fad jet tub

6B
beg cut mix
pox wig fad

6C
bad tug rim
den rob gas

6D
leg fib ham
nut wed fox

6E
cob hem job
pig fad tub

7A
hog dig hum
fad jot gas
beg bad tug
cut leg fib

7B
mix doc bag
rut met rim
den nip jab
hub wed sod

7C
pig nut rag
wed sad gob
rap pin vet
mop lug zip

7D
get bin gum
jab rod yap
cob dim fox
men hug sip

7E
wax leg not
hog yak ten
bus fed rip
sin mug zap

8A
plan span clap
brag clam crab
trap snag bran
slab swam slap

8B
clan flap stab
glad brag snap
scat blab Stan
drab bran cram

8C
drab slap scat
snap snag clan
glad slam brag
trap crab flap

8D
swam trap glad
clap scat blab
drag crab slap
stab snap bran

8E
slab clap swam
plan clam slap
crab snag drab
bran trap Stan

9A
slip skid skip
brim twig grim
slid swim flip
spit drip grid

9B
crib drip skin
clip spin slip
grid slit swim
skip twin flip

9C
swim drip spit
flip slid skip
brim twig grim
grid slip skid

9D
grid swam drip
slap slit clan
crib spam skin
flap twin slam

9E
brim slam grim
twig flap scan
spat drip swam
grad skid slip

10A
frog drop smog
glob trot snob
prod slop blot
crop prom stop

10B
trot prop spot
smog blob slot
prom frog stop
snob drop from

10C
blob drop glob
trot plod stop
crop clod plop
slot flop frog

10D
flop brim plop
swam snob grid
prop spit cram
flag snip brag

10E
brag frog drip
crop grim snag
trot twig stop
flap spit plan

11A
plus smug stub
scum spun slug
snug club glum
stun drum plug

11B
grub scum plug
drum slug glum
spun slum plus
smug club drug

11C
drum snug plum
smug club slug
scum spun stub
plus grub stun

11D
plot prom stub
grub smug trot
spun glob club
plum frog drum

11E
drop plus stun
stub frog plot
trot smug grub
plum club glob

12A
sped glen Fred
sled pled clef
bled stem sled
flex bred fret

12B
Fred step sped
flex fled glen
prep bled bred
pled clef sled

12C
fret sped glen
pled flex sled
bred Fred clef
step fled stem

12D
skin stem prod
plug trip scat
flux drop drum
clan blot fled

12E
grin step skin
plug clip glad
prep bran spot
clog flex grub

13A
thin this flag
step smog thug
then flip them
crop than thus
twin thud that

13B
thus them thug
thud fled brag
snob than crab
then this that
drop thin grip

13C
chat drab sled
grin flop chip
chum Fred chug
swim plug chop
chap frog chin

13D
chap frog chum
plug swim chop
chin spun twig
chug fret chat
chip crab sled

13E
ship slob Glen
that trip shot
shun shop then
flag shin crab
shed stop shut

14A
hush dust rash
song camp help
left dish soft
land gulf bump
with pets film

14B
much hunt math
cast mend link
wish sang honk
Beth fond rush
golf mint sent

14C
push self fang
bang lost went
gift sung math
nest hand rich
king such fond

14D
pest hulk path
ring dash song
both milk dent
damp help musk
gulf pond fish

14E
mask sing bank
rest rush moth
lift band legs
cost mesh cast
dump pink romp

15A
pick lock back
Jack kick neck
puck deck lick
rack luck sack
duck dock tuck

15B
tick Jack pack
duck rack dock
rock buck sick
luck sock yuck
back wick peck

15C
huff yell will
buff tell pill
cuff sell bill
muff fell hill
puff bell fill

15D
putt mess full
mutt less pull
jazz boss mass
fuzz loss pass
buzz moss lass

15E
chip them Jack
mutt trap buzz
skim honk fell
slob mush sled
thug shop grit

16A
dunk clog skit
sped fang hush
bonk grip fret
scan gulf chop
with kept path

16B
drum font crib
vent swam buck
stop chin pelt
raft mutt frog
inch then ramp

16C
bush drop this
stem brag such
moth sick clef
jazz chum golf
wing mess dash

16D
thus chop link
left yank crux
shot fizz then
raft stun dock
pill sent chat

16E
scud lost film
prep snag chug
crop twig tell
swam duck song
thin Beth rash

17A
twist shock
crisp scalp
gruff shelf
slept grass
chunk broth

17B
trend chunk
prong brand
thank flint
press crisp
stump slang

17C
cloth chimp
crust blast
swift flesh
blend slant
thump grump

17D
draft speck
smock gruff
stump swift
stock swept
spill chess

17E
shift slump
clang slept
gloss bless
grand brick
stock skunk

18A
blush frost
thank class
depth cloth
bluff stiff
shift theft

18B
cliff broth
draft spunk
stock shank
tenth shelf
shall spill

18C
slung trend
clasp lunch
pinch blend
scalp frost
bench skill

18D
truck drill
spunk glass
shelf brick
shock press
finch throb

18E
depth thump
floss stuck
theft trash
chimp sloth
thick clang

General Dictation List
Words with Three Letters

Short a:

bad	dab	gas	lag	pal	sag	wag
bag	dad	had	lap	pan	sap	wax
bam	dam	ham	mad	pat	sat	yak
ban	fad	has	man	rag	tab	yam
bat	fan	hat	mat	ram	tag	yap
cab	fat	jab	nab	ran	tan	zap
can	fax	jam	nag	rap	tap	
cap	gab	lab	nap	rat	tax	
cat	gap	lad	pad	sad	van	

Bonus Words: Max, Pam, Sam, and, ant, ask, add

Short e:

bed	fed	jet	let	peg	set	wed
beg	get	keg	men	pen	ten	wet
bet	hem	led	met	pet	vet	yes
den	hen	leg	net	red	web	yet

Bonus Words: Jen, Ken, elf, elk, end, egg

Short i:

bib	dim	gig	kid	pig	sin	win
bid	dip	hid	kit	pin	sip	zip
big	fib	him	lid	pit	sit	
bin	fig	hip	lip	rib	six	
bit	fin	his	lit	rid	tin	
did	fit	hit	mix	rim	tip	
dig	fix	jig	nip	rip	wig	

Bonus Words: Jim, Kim, Tim, ill, ink

Short o:	bog	dot	hog	jot	mom	pop	rot
	box	fog	hop	log	mop	pot	sob
	cob	fox	hot	lop	nod	pox	sod
	cot	gob	job	lot	not	rob	top
	dog	got	jog	mob	pod	rod	tot

Bonus Words: Bob, Tom

Short u:	bud	cud	gum	jug	nub	run	tug
	bug	cup	gut	jut	nun	rut	
	bun	cut	hub	lug	nut	sub	
	bus	dud	hug	mud	pup	sum	
	but	dug	hum	mug	rub	sun	
	cub	fun	hut	mum	rug	tub	

Bonus Word: Gus

Words with Four Letters

Beginning Blends

Short a:	blab	clan	drab	flat	scab	slam	span
	brag	clap	drag	flax	scan	slap	stab
	bran	crab	flag	glad	scat	snag	swam
	clam	cram	flap	plan	slab	snap	trap

Short e:	bled	clef	flex	glen	prep	sped	step
	bred	fled	fret	pled	sled	stem	

Bonus Word: Fred

Short i:	brim	flip	grip	skin	slim	spin	trip
	clip	grid	grit	skip	slip	spit	twig
	crib	grim	skid	skit	slit	swim	twin
	drip	grin	skim	slid	snip	trim	

Short o:	blob	clog	flop	plop	prop	snob
	blog	crop	frog	plot	slop	spot
	blot	drop	glob	prod	slot	stop
	clod	flog	plod	prom	smog	trot

Short u:	club	flub	grub	scum	snug	stud
	crux	flux	plug	slug	spud	stun
	drug	glum	plum	slum	spun	
	drum	glut	plus	smug	stub	

Digraphs

| **ch:** | chap | chat | chin | chip | chop | chug | chum |

| **sh:** | sham | shin | shop | shun |
| | shed | ship | shot | shut |

| **th:** | than | them | thin | thud | thus |
| | that | then | this | thug | |

End Blends

Short a:	band	cast	fang	lamp	mast	ramp	sank
	bang	cats	fast	land	pant	rang	tank
	bank	damp	gang	last	past	sand	task
	camp	fact	hand	mask	raft	sang	yank

Short e:	beds	desk	hens	lets	pens	sets	vets
	begs	eggs	jest	melt	pent	tend	weld
	belt	felt	jets	mend	pest	tens	welt
	bend	fend	kelp	nest	pets	tent	went
	bent	gets	kept	nets	rent	test	wept
	best	held	left	next	rest	text	west
	bets	helm	legs	pegs	self	vend	wets
	dens	help	lend	pelt	send	vent	yelp
	dent	hems	lent	pend	sent	vest	zest

Bonus Word: Kent

Short i:	ding	hint	link	mint	rink	sink	wing
	film	kilt	lint	mist	risk	tilt	wink
	fist	king	list	ping	sift	tint	
	gift	lift	milk	pink	silk	wilt	
	hilt	limp	mink	ring	sing	wind	

Short o:	bond	fond	gong	lost	pond	rots	tong
	bonk	font	honk	lots	pots	soft	tops
	cost	golf	long	pomp	romp	song	tots

Short u:	bulb	cuts	gulf	hunk	lung	rung	sulk
	bulk	duct	gulp	hunt	musk	runs	sung
	bump	dump	gunk	husk	must	runt	sunk
	bunk	dunk	gust	jump	nuts	rust	tuft
	bust	dusk	hulk	junk	pump	scud	tusk
	cups	dust	hump	just	rugs	slug	
	cusp	fund	hung	lump	rump	suds	

Digraphs

ch:	inch	rich	much	such			

sh:	dash	rash	dish	wish	gush	lush	rush
	mash	mesh	fish	josh	hush	mush	

th:	bath	math	path	with	moth	Beth	

Double Consonants at End

ff:	buff	cuff	huff	muff	puff	ruff	

ll:	bell	jell	well	dill	kill	doll	hull
	dell	sell	yell	fill	pill	dull	lull
	fell	tell	bill	hill	will	gull	mull

ss:	lass	pass	mess	miss	loss	toss
	mass	less	kiss	boss	moss	fuss

tt:	putt	mutt

zz:	jazz	razz	fizz	buzz	fuzz

ck:	back	sack	peck	sick	lock	duck	tuck
	jack	tack	kick	tick	rock	luck	yuck
	pack	deck	lick	wick	sock	muck	
	rack	neck	pick	dock	buck	puck	

Five-Letter Words

Short a:	blank	clang	crank	grant	scalp	stamp
	blast	clasp	draft	grasp	scamp	stand
	brand	craft	drank	plank	slang	tramp
	clamp	cramp	grand	plant	slant	

Short e:	blend	crest	shelf	spend	swept
	crept	flesh	slept	spent	trend

Short i:	blink	cling	drink	print	sting	swing
	bring	crisp	fling	sling	stink	twist
	brisk	drift	flint	slink	swift	

Short o:	frost	prong	stomp

Short u:	blunt	crust	grunt	skunk	spunk	stunt
	clump	drunk	plump	slump	stump	trunk
	clung	grump	plunk	slung	stung	trust

Five-Letter Words with Digraphs

Note: the short vowel is not always in the middle position

ch:	bunch	check	chimp	hunch	munch	ranch	
	champ	chest	chunk	lunch	pinch		
	chant	chick	finch	mulch	punch		

sh:	shack	shank	brash	flash	flesh	brush	plush
	shaft	shelf	clash	smash	swish	crush	
	shall	shift	crash	trash	blush	flush	

th:	thank	thing	thump	fifth	width	froth	
	theft	think	depth	filth	broth	sloth	
	thick	throb	tenth	sixth	cloth		

ck:	black	check	cluck	flick	shock	stick	track
	brick	click	crock	flock	smock	stock	trick
	block	clock	fleck	pluck	speck	stuck	truck

Double Consonant Endings

bless	chess	cross	fluff	grill	sniff	stuff
bliss	chill	dress	glass	gruff	spill	truss
bluff	class	drill	gloss	press	stiff	
brass	cliff	floss	grass	skill	still	

Bonus Word: Swiss

Passages for Dictation

19 I'm a little teapot,

Short and stout.

Here is my handle,

Here is my spout.

When I get all steamed up,

Hear me shout.

Then tip me over

And pour me out!

20 Little Bo Peep has lost her sheep

And doesn't know where to find them.

Leave them alone, and they'll come home,

Wagging their tails behind them.

21 The itsy, bitsy spider went up the water spout.

Down came the rain and washed the spider out.

Out came the sun and dried up all the rain,

And the itsy, bitsy spider went up the spout again.

22 Old Mother Hubbard

Went to her cupboard

To get her poor dog a bone.

But when she got there,

Her cupboard was bare,

And so the poor dog had none.

23 Tom, he was a piper's son.

He learned to play when he was young,

But the only tune that he could play

Was "Over the Hills and Far Away."

24 Roses are red.

Violets are blue.

Sugar is sweet,

And so are you.

25 Little Boy Blue,

Come blow your horn.

The sheep's in the meadow.

The cow's in the corn.

But where is the little boy

Who looks after the sheep?

He's under the haystack, fast asleep!

26 Star light, star bright,

First star I see tonight,

I wish I may, I wish I might

Have the wish I wish tonight.

27 There once was a jolly miller

Who lived on the river Dee.

He worked and sang from morn till night,

No lark more happy than he.

28 Jenny Wren was slowly flying
Over the hills sadly crying,
"Have you seen my lovely locket?
I've searched, and I cannot find it."

29 Hickory, dickory, dock,
The mouse ran up the clock.
The clock struck one.
The mouse ran down.
Hickory, dickory, dock.

30 A wise old owl lived in an oak.
The more he saw the less he spoke.
The less he spoke the more he heard.
When he spoke 'twas a thoughtful word.

31 This old man, he played one,
He played knick-knack on his thumb.
With a knick-knack paddy whack,
Give the dog a bone.
This old man came rolling home!

32 One, two, buckle my shoe.
Three, four, shut the door.
Five, six, pick up sticks.
Seven, eight, lay them straight.
Nine, ten, big fat hen.

33 This little piggy went to market.

This little piggy stayed home.

This little piggy had roast beef.

This little piggy had none.

This little piggy cried,

"Wee, wee, wee, wee, wee,"

All the way home.

34 Humpty Dumpty sat on a wall.

Humpty Dumpty had a great fall.

All the king's horses

And all the king's men

Couldn't put Humpty together again.

35 There was an old lady who swallowed a fly.

I don't know why she swallowed the fly.

I guess she'll die.

There was an old lady who swallowed a spider

That wiggled and jiggled and tickled inside her.

She swallowed the spider to catch the fly.

I don't know why she swallowed the fly.

I guess she'll die.

36 Old MacDonald had a farm, E I E I O.

And on his farm he had some ducks, E I E I O.

With a quack, quack here and a quack, quack there,

Here a quack, there a quack, everywhere a quack, quack.

Old MacDonald had a farm, E I E I O!

Old MacDonald had a farm, E I E I O.
And on his farm he had some chickens, E I E I O.
With a cluck, cluck here and a cluck, cluck there,
Here a cluck, there a cluck, everywhere a cluck, cluck.
Old MacDonald had a farm, E I E I O!

Old MacDonald had a farm, E I E I O.
And on his farm he had some cows, E I E I O.
With a moo, moo here and a moo, moo there,
Here a moo, there a moo, everywhere a moo, moo.
Old MacDonald had a farm, E I E I O!

Old MacDonald had a farm, E I E I O.
And on his farm he had some sheep, E I E I O.
With a baa, baa here and a baa, baa there,
Here a baa, there a baa, everywhere a baa, baa.
Old MacDonald had a farm, E I E I O!

Old MacDonald had a farm, E I E I O.
And on his farm he had a dog, E I E I O.
With a woof, woof here and a woof, woof there,
Here a woof, there a woof, everywhere a woof, woof.
Old MacDonald had a farm, E I E I O!

Answer Key

1A: *Jill* and *hill* should be underlined.

1B: *Jack* and *Jill* should be underlined (2 times).

1C: Two periods and one comma should be circled.

1D: *Jack* and *Jill* should be underlined (2 times).

1E: The word *crown* (or *his crown*) should be underlined.

2A: The first letter of each line (*T, R, T, A*) should be circled.

2B: The word *round* should be underlined (8 times).

2C: The word *swish* should be underlined (12 times).

2D: The word *horn* should be underlined (2 times). The word *honk* should be underlined (12 times).

2E: The word *The/the* should be underlined (5 times). The words *through* and *town* should each be underlined.

3A: The first letter of each line (*R, G, M, L*) should be circled.

3B: Six commas and two periods should be circled.

3C: The word *merrily* should be underlined (4 times).

3D: The words *stream* and *dream* should be underlined.

3E: The word *down* should be underlined.

4A: *Diddle, fiddle, moon,* and *spoon* should be underlined.

4B: The word *fiddle* should be underlined.

4C: The *-ed* endings in the words *jumped* and *laughed* should be marked in pink or red.

4D: The words *cat, cow,* and *dog* should be underlined.

4E: The word *The/the* should be underlined (7 times).

5A: The first letter of each line (*B, H, Y, O, A, A, W*) should be circled.

5B: Four quotation marks should be circled.

5C: The word *three* should be underlined (1 time), and the word *one* should be underlined (3 times).

5D: The words *wool* and *full* should be underlined.

5E: The word *yes* should be underlined (two times).

6A: The word *up* should be underlined.

6B: The *-ing* endings in the words *raining, pouring, snoring,* and *morning* should be marked in pink or red.

6C: The word *bed* should be underlined.

6D: The *-ed* ending in the word *bumped* should be marked in pink or red.

6E: The words *It's/it's* (2 times) and *couldn't* (1 time) should be underlined.

7A: One comma and two periods should be circled.

7B: The words *snow* and *go* should be underlined.

7C: The first letter of each line (*M, I, A, T*) and the *M* in *Mary* in the third line should be circled.

7D: The word *little* should be underlined.

7E: The words *white, went,* and *was* (2 times) should be underlined.

8A: The letter *a* occurs 11 times and should be circled each time.

8B: The letter *i* occurs eight times and should be circled each time.

8C: The letter *e* occurs 12 times and should be circled each time.

8D: Two commas, four quotation marks, one question mark, and one period should be circled.

8E: The letter *o* occurs nine times and should be circled each time.

9A: The letter *r* occurs seven times and should be circled each time.

9B: The following words have Bossy *r* chunks that should be marked in purple: *star, wonder, are*, and *world*.

9C: The following words have a silent *e* at the end that should be marked in orange: *twinkle* (4 times), *little* (2 times), *are* (2 times), *above*, and *like*.

9D: Seven commas and three periods should be circled.

9E: The pairs of rhyming words are *star* and *are (2 times)* and *high* and *sky*.

10A: The double consonants *tt* in *Little, ff* in *Muffet* (2 times), *ss* in *Miss* (2 times), and *ff* in *tuffet* should be marked in blue.

10B: The *-ing* in *eating* and *-ed* in *frightened* should be marked in pink or red.

10C: Every word in the rhyme has at least one vowel. The letter *a* occurs 11 times, *e* occurs 14 times, *i* occurs seven times, *o* occurs four times, and *u* occurs four times. Each vowel should be circled.

10D: The first letter of each line (*L, S, E, A, W, A*) and the *M* in *Miss* and *Muffet* (2 times each) should be circled.

10E: The pairs of rhyming words are *Muffet* and *tuffet, whey* and *away, spider* and *her*.

11A: The vowel chunks are *ow* in *down, oo* in *looked, oa* in *coat, ou* in *our* and *you*, and *ie* in *friend*.

11B: The *-ed* in *walked* and *looked* should be marked in pink or red.

11C: The *ck* in *ducklings* should be marked in blue.

11D: Three periods, three commas, four quotation marks, and one question mark should be circled.

11E: The *l* in *walked* should be marked in orange.

12A: Six exclamation points should be circled.

12B: The following words have a silent *e* at the end that should be marked in orange: *Pease* (3 times), *porridge* (3 times), *nine* (2 times), *some* (3 times), and *like* (3 times).

12C: The opposites are *hot* and *cold*.

12D: The double consonants *rr* in *porridge* (3 times) should be marked in blue.

12E: The *P* in *Pease* and the *S* in *Some* (3 times each) should be circled.

13A: The pairs of rhyming words are *rye* and *pie*, *sing* and *king*.

13B: Tricky *y* is in *rye*, *twenty*, and *dainty*. Tricky *y* should be marked in green.

13C: The *-ed* in *baked* and *opened* should be marked in pink or red.

13D: Three commas, two periods, and one question mark should be circled.

13E: The word *Wasn't* should be underlined.

14A: Tricky *y* is in *Banbury*, *Tommy*, and *penny* (3 times). It is not counted in the vowel chunk *uy*, found in *buy*. Tricky *y* should be marked in green.

14B: The double consonants *ss* in *Cross*, *mm* in *Tommy*, *nn* in *penny* (3 times), and *pp* in *apple* should be marked in blue.

14C: The first letter of each line (*R*, *T*, *A*, *A*, *A*), the *B* in *Banbury*, the *C* in *Cross*, and the *T* in *Tommy* should be circled.

14D: The colon (:) after *buy* should be circled.

14E: Bossy *r* is in *horse* and *Banbury*.

15A: There are two Bossy *r* chunks in *Horner* and two in *corner*.

15B: The *-ing* in *eating* and *-ed* in *pulled* should be marked in pink or red.

15C: The silent *e* in *Little* and the silent *b* in *thumb* should be marked in orange.

15D: The vowel chunks are *Ea* in *Eating*, *ie* in *pie*, *ou* in *out*, *ai* in *said*, *oo* in *good*, and *oy* in *boy*.

15E: There are two quotation marks in the last line of the rhyme.

16A: The *ck* in *black*, *tch* in *matching*, and *ck* in *ducks* should be marked in blue.

16B: The rhyming words at the ends of the lines are *hats/flats* and *boots/suits*.

16C: The Bossy *r* chunk is *er* in *powdered*.

16D: One comma and two periods should be circled.

16E: The *-ing* in *matching* should be marked in pink or red.

17A: The vowel chunks are *oa* in coal, *ai* in *said*, and *ou* in *you*.

17B: The double consonants *tt* in *little* occur three times.

17C: Tricky *y* Guy is in *by* and *why*.

17D: There are two quotation marks in the last line of the rhyme.

17E: The Bossy *r* chunks are *ir* in *fire*, *er* in *over*, *er* in *fender*, and *er* in *other*.

18A: The consonant chunk *ck* is in *Jack* (3 times), *quick*, and *candlestick*.

18B: The capital *J* in *Jack* occurs three times. The last line begins with a capital *T*.

18C: The silent *e* is at the end of *nimble*.

18D: The consonant chunk *ck* is in *Jack* (3 times), *quick*, and *candlestick*.

18E: Two commas and one exclamation point should be circled.

Sometimes a word has overlapping chunks. For example, a vowel chunk may overlap with a Bossy *r* chunk (*heard*), or a consonant chunk may overlap with an ending (*really*). In the answer key, we have tried to remain consistent with the focus of each lesson. In lessons with multiple chunks, we marked vowel chunks before Bossy *r* chunks and Bossy *r* chunks before consonant chunks.

If the student chooses a different chunking pattern than the one marked in the answer key, please do not consider it incorrect. Instead, take a moment to talk about the word and the overlap of chunks. You might ask the student which letter pattern he thinks would be most helpful for him to remember and let him mark that one. Remember that the goal is to create a visual memory for non-phonetic words.

19. I'm a little teapot,

 Short and stout.

 Here is my handle,

 Here is my spout.

 When I get all steamed up,

 Hear me shout.

 Then tip me over

 And pour me out!

 Vowel Chunks: 8

20. Little Bo Peep has lost her sheep

    And doesn't know where to find them.

    Leave them alone, and they'll come home,

    Wagging their tails behind them.

    Vowel Chunks: 8   **Silent Letters: 6**

21. The itsy, bitsy spider went up the water spout.

    Down came the rain and washed the spider out.

    Out came the sun and dried up all the rain,

    And the itsy, bitsy spider went up the spout again.

    Vowel Chunks: 9   **Tricky y Guy: 4**

22. Old Mother Hubbard

    Went to her cupboard

    To get her poor dog a bone.

    But when she got there,

    Her cupboard was bare,

    And so the poor dog had none.

    Bossy r Chunks: 11

23. Tom, he was a piper's son.

    He learned to play when he was young,

    But the only tune that he could play

    Was "Over the Hills and Far Away."

    Vowel Chunks: 6 (Technically the *aw* in *Away* is not a vowel chunk because the letters are in two different syllables. You may decide whether or not to make this distinction with your student.)

24. Roses are red.

    Violets are blue.

    Sugar is sweet,

    And so are you.

    Vowel Chunks: 4   **Bossy r Chunks: 4**

25. Little Boy Blue,

    Come blow your horn.

    The sheep's in the meadow.

    The cow's in the corn.

    But where is the little boy

    Who looks after the sheep?

    He's under the haystack, fast asleep!

    Vowel Chunks: 13   **Bossy r Chunks: 5**

26. Star light, star bright,

    First star I see tonight.

    I wish I may, I wish I might

    Have the wish I wish tonight.

    Consonant Chunks: 10

27. There once was a jolly miller

    Who lived on the river Dee.

    He worked and sang from morn till night,

    No lark more happy than he.

    Consonant Chunks: 9

28. Jenny Wren was slowly flying
    Over the hills sadly crying,
    "Have you seen my lovely locket?
    I've searched, and I cannot find it."

    Consonant Chunks: 7   **Endings: 6**

29. Hickory, dickory, dock,
    The mouse ran up the clock.
    The clock struck one.
    The mouse ran down.
    Hickory, dickory, dock.

    Consonant Chunks: 13   **Tricky y Guy: 4**

30. A wise old owl lived in an oak.
    The more he saw the less he spoke.
    The less he spoke the more he heard.
    When he spoke 'twas a thoughtful word.

    Vowel Chunks: 5   **Consonant Chunks: 9**

31. This old man, he played one,
    He played knick-knack on his thumb.
    With a knick-knack paddy whack,
    Give the dog a bone.
    This old man came rolling home!

    Consonant Chunks: 17   **Silent Letters: 6**

32. One, two, buckle my shoe.

 Three, four, shut the door.

 Five, six, pick up sticks.

 Seven, eight, lay them straight.

 Nine, ten, big fat hen.

 Consonant Chunks: 10   **Silent Letters: 4**

33. This little piggy went to market.

 This little piggy stayed home.

 This little piggy had roast beef.

 This little piggy had none.

 This little piggy cried,

 "Wee, wee, wee, wee, wee,"

 All the way home.

 Consonant Chunks: 17   **Silent Letters: 8**   **Tricky y Guy: 5**

34. Humpty Dumpty sat on a wall.

 Humpty Dumpty had a great fall.

 All the king's horses

 And all the king's men

 Couldn't put Humpty together again.

 Vowel Chunks: 3   **Tricky y Guy: 5**

35. There was an old lady who swallowed a fly.

    I don't know why she swallowed the fly.

    I guess she'll die.

    There was an old lady who swallowed a spider

    That wiggled and jiggled and tickled inside her.

    She swallowed the spider to catch the fly.

    I don't know why she swallowed the fly.

    I guess she'll die.

    Vowel Chunks: 11   **Tricky y Guy: 8**   **Endings: 8**

36. Old MacDonald had a farm, E I E I O.

    And on his farm he had some ducks, E I E I O.

    With a quack, quack here and a quack, quack there,

    Here a quack, there a quack, everywhere a quack, quack.

    Old MacDonald had a farm, E I E I O!

    Consonant Chunks: 21   **Bossy r Chunks: 9**   **Silent Letters: 6**

    Old MacDonald had a farm, E I E I O.

    And on his farm he had some chickens, E I E I O.

    With a cluck, cluck here and a cluck, cluck there,

    Here a cluck, there a cluck, everywhere a cluck, cluck.

    Old MacDonald had a farm, E I E I O!

    Consonant Chunks: 14   **Bossy r Chunks: 9**   **Silent Letters: 6**

Old MacDonald had a farm, E I E I O.

And on his farm he had some cows, E I E I O.

With a moo, moo here and a moo, moo there,

Here a moo, there a moo, everywhere a moo, moo.

Old MacDonald had a farm, E I E I O!

Consonant Chunks: 4   **Bossy _r_ Chunks: 9**   **Silent Letters: 6**

Old MacDonald had a farm, E I E I O.

And on his farm he had some sheep, E I E I O.

With a baa, baa here and a baa, baa there,

Here a baa, there a baa, everywhere a baa, baa.

Old MacDonald had a farm, E I E I O!

Consonant Chunks: 5   **Bossy _r_ Chunks: 9**   **Silent Letters: 6**

Old MacDonald had a farm, E I E I O.

And on his farm he had a dog, E I E I O.

With a woof, woof here and a woof, woof there,

Here a woof, there a woof, everywhere a woof, woof.

Old MacDonald had a farm, E I E I O!

Consonant Chunks: 4   **Bossy _r_ Chunks: 9**   **Silent Letters: 5**

Glossary

Blend – two or more consonants that appear together but keep their distinct sounds. Words like *flag, stop,* and *stream* begin with blends, and the word *fast* ends with a blend. A blend is different than a consonant chunk because all the sounds of the consonants are heard.

Bossy r – a letter pattern in which a vowel is followed by an *r* that controls ("bosses") the vowel by changing its sound

Chunk – a particular letter pattern that occurs frequently in English and which may not have a predictable sound

Chunking – the process of finding and marking all the designated letter patterns in a particular passage

Consonant – any letter of the alphabet that is not a vowel. The consonants are *b, c, d, f, g, h, j, k, l, m, n, p, q, r, s, t, v, w, x, y,* and *z*.

Consonant chunks – a combination of two or more consonants that usually make a single sound. Consonant chunks may also be silent.

Copywork – words or sentences provided for a student to copy

Decode – use letter-to-sound correspondence to read a word in print. This is the skill students practice when they read the words back at the end of a dictation.

Dictation – the process of reading a sentence or passage aloud and having the student write it without looking at the passage

Encode – create a word from individual sounds. Students practice this skill during dictation when they write individual letters to match the sounds they hear.

High-frequency words – the most commonly-used words, such as *the, and,* or *but*

Phonemic awareness – the ability to distinguish the individual sounds that make up spoken words

Phonics – the study of the sounds usually indicated by letters and combinations of letters in a particular language

Preliterate – the developmental stage of spelling at which children begin to become familiar with the idea of written language

Sight words – high-frequency words that are non-phonetic and, as a result, especially challenging for emerging readers. Examples are *come, look, of, said*, and *some*.

Silent letter – a letter that is included when spelling a word but has no sound when the word is pronounced

Syllable – a word or part of a word pronounced as a single unit. It consists of one vowel sound and often the consonant sounds that cluster around it.

Tricky y Guy – a *y* in the middle or at the end of a word that is sounded as a vowel instead of as a consonant

Vowel – one of the letters *a, e, i, o,* and *u*. Sometimes *y* and *w* also act as vowels. Every syllable and word in the English language has at least one vowel sound.

Vowel chunks – a combination of two or more vowels. A vowel chunk usually has a single sound.

Bibliography

This curriculum is based on years of research into how children learn to read and spell. Here are some of the resources that were used in the development of this program.

Berk, L. E., & Winsler, A. (1995). *Scaffolding children's learning: Vygotsky and early childhood education.* Washington, DC: National Association for the Education of Young Children.

Clay, M. M. (1991). *Becoming literate: The construction of inner control.* Portsmouth, NH: Heinemann.

Clay, M. M. (2010). *What changes in writing can I see?* Portsmouth, NH: Heinemann.

Cook, D. L. (2004). *When your child struggles: The myths of 20/20 vision: What every parent needs to know.* Atlanta, GA: Invision Press.

Cunningham, P. M. (2012). *Phonics they use: Words for reading and writing* (6th ed.). New York, NY: Pearson.

Flanigan, K., Hayes, L., Templeton, S., Bear, D. R., Invernizzi, M. R., & Johnston, F. (2011). *Words their way with struggling readers: Word study for reading, vocabulary, and spelling instruction, grades 4–12.* Boston, MA: Allyn & Bacon.

Fountas, I. C., & Pinnell, G. S. (Eds). (1999). *Voices on word matters: Learning about phonics and spelling in the literacy classroom.* Portsmouth, NH: Heinemann.

Ganske, K. (2008). *Mindful of words: Spelling and vocabulary explorations 4–8 (Solving problems in teaching of literacy).* New York, NY: Guilford Press.

Heilman, A. W. (1968). *Phonics in proper perspective.* (2nd ed.). Columbus, OH: Charles E. Merrill Publishing Company.

Henderson, E. H. (1990). *Teaching spelling* (2nd ed.). Boston, MA: Houghton Mifflin.

Levine, M. (2000). *Educational care: A system for understanding and helping children with learning differences at home and in school* (2nd ed.). Cambridge, MA: Educators Publishing Service.

Lyons, C. A. (2003). *Teaching struggling readers: How to use brain-based research to maximize learning.* Portsmouth, NH: Heinemann.

McCarrier, A., Pinnell, G. S., & Fountas, I. C. (2000). *Interactive writing: How language and literacy come together, K–2.* Portsmouth, NH: Heinemann.

Pinnell, G. S., & Fountas, I. C. (1998). *Word matters: Teaching phonics and spelling in the reading/writing classroom.* Portsmouth, NH: Heinemann.

Read, C. (1971). Pre-school children's knowledge of English phonology. *Harvard Educational Review,* 41(1), 150–179.

Sprenger, M. (1999). *Learning and memory: The brain in action.* Alexandria, VA: Association for Supervision and Curriculum Development.

Wood, D. (1988). *How children think and learn: The social contexts of cognitive development.* Cambridge, MA: Blackwell Publishers.

Zutell, J. (1998). Word sorting: A developmental spelling approach to word study for delayed readers. *Reading and Writing Quarterly,* 14(2), 219–238.

JAN 202 **DATE DUE**

PRINTED IN U.S.A.